THE ART OF CLASSROOM MANAGEMENT

THE ART OF CLASSROOM MANAGEMENT

Providing Effective Classroom
Management Strategies

NATASHA CARTER

McClure Publishing, Inc.

Copyright © 2024 – Natasha Carter at McClure Publishing, Inc.

All rights reserved. Printed and bound in the United States of America. According to the 1976 United States Copyright Act, no part of this book may be reproduced or utilized in any form or by any means, electronic or mechanical, including photocopying, recording, or by any information storage or retrieval system, except by a reviewer who may quote brief passages in a review to be printed in a magazine or newspaper, without permission in writing from the Publisher: Inquiries should be addressed to McClure Publishing, Inc. Permissions Department, 398 West Army Trail Road, Bloomingdale, IL 60108. First Printing: June 29, 2024.

ISBN-13: 979-8-9907047-1-8

Book cover designed by Natasha Carter

To order additional copies, please contact:

McClure Publishing, Inc.
https://McClurePublishing.com
800.659.4908

MANUAL DESCRIPTION:

This concise manual introduces practical and effective classroom management strategies for teachers and educators. Participants will gain hands-on techniques to establish a positive, productive learning environment and enhance student engagement and success.

WHO IS THIS MANUAL FOR?

This manual is designed for:

- ❖ New or aspiring teachers
- ❖ Current teachers looking to improve their classroom management skills
- ❖ School administrators and instructional coaches
- ❖ Anyone interested in developing effective classroom management practices

MANUAL LEARNING OUTCOMES:

By the end of this manual, participants will be able to:

1. Establish clear classroom rules, routines, and procedures to promote order and structure.
2. Implement proactive strategies to prevent and address disruptive student behaviors.
3. Utilize positive reinforcement and behavior management techniques to encourage student cooperation and motivation.
4. Develop effective communication and relationship-building skills with students.
5. Create an inclusive, supportive learning environment that meets the diverse needs of all students.

TABLE OF CONTENTS

INTRODUCTION

CHAPTER 1: INTRODUCTION TO CLASSROOM MANAGEMENT 13

UNDERSTANDING THE IMPORTANCE OF EFFECTIVE CLASSROOM MANAGEMENT 13
DEFINING KEY TERMS 15
EXPLORING DIFFERENT APPROACHES 16
QUIZ 18

CHAPTER 2: ESTABLISHING A POSITIVE CLASSROOM 20

CREATING A WELCOMING AND INCLUSIVE CLASSROOM CULTURE 20
BUILDING POSITIVE RELATIONSHIPS WITH STUDENTS 21
PROMOTING MUTUAL RESPECT AND COOPERATION 22
QUIZ 24

CHAPTER 3: DEVELOPING CLASSROOM RULES AND PROCEDURES 26

SETTING CLEAR EXPECTATIONS AND RULES 26
TEACHING AND REINFORCING CLASSROOM PROCEDURES ...27
ADDRESSING RULE VIOLATIONS AND CONSEQUENCES 28
QUIZ 30

CHAPTER 4: EFFECTIVE LESSON PLANNING AND INSTRUCTION ...32

DESIGNING ENGAGING AND WELL-STRUCTURED LESSONS ...32
INCORPORATING DIFFERENT TEACHING STRATEGIES AND TECHNIQUES 33
MANAGING TRANSITIONS AND MAXIMIZING INSTRUCTIONAL TIME 34
QUIZ 36

CHAPTER 5: MANAGING STUDENT BEHAVIOR 38

IDENTIFYING AND ADDRESSING CHALLENGING BEHAVIORS ...38
IMPLEMENTING PROACTIVE STRATEGIES FOR BEHAVIOR MANAGEMENT 39

USING POSITIVE REINFORCEMENT AND EFFECTIVE DISCIPLINE
TECHNIQUES 40
QUIZ 42

CHAPTER 6: PROMOTING STUDENT ENGAGEMENT AND PARTICIPATION 44

CREATING A STIMULATING LEARNING ENVIRONMENT 44
ENCOURAGING ACTIVE LEARNING AND STUDENT INVOLVEMENT . 45
DIFFERENTIATING INSTRUCTION TO MEET DIVERSE STUDENT
NEEDS 47
QUIZ 49

CHAPTER 7: CLASSROOM ORGANIZATION AND MATERIALS MANAGEMENT 51

ARRANGING THE PHYSICAL SPACE FOR OPTIMAL LEARNING 51
MANAGING CLASSROOM RESOURCES AND MATERIALS 52
UTILIZING TECHNOLOGY EFFECTIVELY IN THE CLASSROOM 54
QUIZ 56

CHAPTER 8: EFFECTIVE COMMUNICATION AND COLLABORATION 58

ESTABLISHING OPEN LINES OF COMMUNICATION WITH STUDENTS
AND PARENTS 58
FOSTERING A COLLABORATIVE CLASSROOM COMMUNITY 60
RESOLVING CONFLICTS AND ADDRESSING CONCERNS 61
QUIZ 63

CHAPTER 9: BUILDING EFFECTIVE CLASSROOM ROUTINES 65

ESTABLISHING CONSISTENT DAILY ROUTINES AND PROCEDURES . 65
MANAGING TRANSITIONS AND DISRUPTIONS 66
PROMOTING STUDENT INDEPENDENCE AND RESPONSIBILITY 68
QUIZ 70

CHAPTER 10: REFLECTING AND GROWING AS A CLASSROOM
MANAGER 72
REFLECTING ON TEACHING PRACTICES AND CLASSROOM
MANAGEMENT STRATEGIES 72

SEEKING FEEDBACK AND PROFESSIONAL DEVELOPMENT
   OPPORTUNITIES 73
DEVELOPING A PERSONAL ACTION PLAN FOR CONTINUOUS
   IMPROVEMENT 74

QUIZ 76

CONCLUSION 78

ANSWER KEY

INTRODUCTION

Effective classroom management is essential for creating a productive, engaging learning environment where students can thrive. Classroom management encompasses all the decisions and actions teachers take to foster students' social, emotional, and academic development.

From establishing clear expectations and routines to cultivating positive relationships with students to implementing behavior intervention strategies, classroom management requires a multi-faceted approach. When done well, it enables teachers to spend more time on instruction and less time dealing with disruptions.

This manual will equip you with research-based principles and practical techniques for managing your classroom effectively. You'll learn strategies to prevent misbehavior, respond appropriately when issues arise, and create a climate that supports student learning and wellbeing. With the right classroom management skills, you can maximize instructional time, enhance student engagement, and facilitate academic success for all.

CHAPTER 1: INTRODUCTION TO CLASSROOM MANAGEMENT

LESSON OBJECTIVE

At the end of this chapter, participants will be able to understand the following:

- Understanding the importance of effective classroom management
- Defining key terms and concepts
- Exploring different approaches to classroom management

UNDERSTANDING THE IMPORTANCE OF EFFECTIVE CLASSROOM MANAGEMENT

Classroom management is one of the most critical skills for teachers to develop and master. It encompasses the decisions, actions, and strategies used to establish and maintain an orderly, productive learning environment. Effective classroom management is essential for maximizing instructional time, supporting student learning and wellbeing, and creating a positive school climate.

At its core, classroom management involves more than just controlling student behavior. It involves proactively structuring the classroom, cultivating positive teacher-student relationships, and fostering student self-regulation and engagement. When implemented effectively, it can have a profound impact on academic achievement, social-emotional development, and overall school success.

ESTABLISHING ORDER AND STRUCTURE

One key aim of classroom management is to create a calm, organized learning space. Teachers skilled at classroom management establish clear rules, routines, and procedures that promote order and predictability. This minimizes disruptions, increases on-task behavior, and allows more time for teaching and learning.

When students understand classroom expectations, they feel secure and can better focus on academic tasks. Establishing structure also helps teachers anticipate and prevent behavior issues before they escalate. With a well-managed classroom, teachers can redirect minor misbehaviors quickly and efficiently.

SUPPORTING STUDENT ENGAGEMENT AND MOTIVATION

Beyond controlling conduct, effective classroom management nurtures student investment and intrinsic motivation. By implementing engaging lessons, offering choice, and using positive reinforcement, teachers can foster a classroom environment that sparks students' natural curiosity and love of learning.

When students are meaningfully engaged, they are less likely to act out or become disruptive. Engagement also supports the development of critical self-regulation skills as students learn to manage their own behavior and emotions. This promotes autonomy, productivity, and a sense of community—all essential for academic success.

CULTIVATING POSITIVE RELATIONSHIPS

At its heart, classroom management is about building caring, trust-based relationships between teachers and students. Effective teachers understand that positive interactions, empathy, and mutual respect are foundational. When students feel known, valued, and supported, they are more likely to cooperate, be motivated, and thrive.

Strong teacher-student relationships also enable teachers to better anticipate and respond to student needs. This allows them to provide the right level of structure, scaffolding, and support to help each student succeed. Positive relationships also lay the groundwork for successful behavior intervention when issues do arise.

PROMOTING INCLUSIVE, EQUITABLE LEARNING

Classroom management plays a vital role in creating learning environments that are inclusive and responsive to student diversity. Effective management strategies help ensure all students, regardless of background or learning profile, feel safe, respected, and able to fully participate.

This might involve implementing Universal Design for Learning principles, differentiating instruction, and using culturally responsive teaching practices. It also means proactively addressing implicit biases and other obstacles to inclusion. When classroom management fosters a climate of acceptance and belonging, it supports the academic and social-emotional wellbeing of all students.

DEFINING KEY TERMS

To fully understand the significance of classroom management, it's important to define some key concepts:

1. Behavior management refers to the strategies and techniques used to address student misbehavior, such as redirecting, using consequences, and teaching replacement behaviors.

2. Classroom climate encompasses the overall tone, attitudes, and interpersonal dynamics present. A positive climate is marked by warmth, safety, and a sense of community.
3. Student engagement speaks to the level of attention, interest, and active participation students demonstrate during lessons.
4. Self-regulation is the ability to manage one's own behavior, emotions, and learning processes—a critical skill supporting academic and social-emotional development.
5. Differentiation involves tailoring instruction and support to meet the diverse needs and learning profiles of students.
6. Culturally responsive teaching builds upon students' cultural backgrounds and life experiences.

EXPLORING DIFFERENT APPROACHES

There is no single approach to classroom management. Effective teachers draw from a range of philosophies, models, and techniques to create a customized approach for their unique context.

Some common approaches include:

1. **Behaviorist Approaches:** Using positive and negative reinforcement to shape student behavior, such as token economies and behavior contracts.
2. **Authoritative Approaches:** Establishing clear expectations while also providing high levels of emotional support and responsiveness.
3. **Relationship-Based Approaches:** Centering around building strong, caring connections between teachers and students.

4. **Restorative Practices:** Emphasizing repairing harm, resolving conflicts, and restoring relationships when behavior issues arise.
5. **Collaborative Approaches:** Actively involving students in creating classroom norms and decision-making.
6. Successful classroom management requires a dynamic, multi-faceted approach tailored to the needs of students, curriculum, and environment. By drawing from diverse strategies and philosophies, teachers can create orderly, engaging classrooms that support the learning and development of all students.

QUIZ

1. What is the primary aim of establishing clear rules, routines, and procedures in the classroom?

    A. To control student behavior

    B. To maximize instructional time

    C. To foster student self-regulation

    D. All of the above

2. Which of the following is NOT a key benefit of effective classroom management?

    A. Increased student engagement

    B. Improved academic achievement

    C. Reduced teacher stress

    D. Enhanced student social-emotional development

3. Which of the following classroom management approaches emphasizes building strong, caring relationships between teachers and students?

    A. Behaviorist approach

    B. Authoritative approach

    C. Relationship-based approach

    D. Restorative practices

4. What is the primary purpose of differentiation in the context of classroom management?

    A. To ensure all students are treated equally

    B. To promote student independence

C. To meet the diverse needs of all students

D. To minimize behavior issues

5. Which of the following is a key component of culturally responsive teaching in the classroom?

      A. Implementing strict behavior policies

      B. Focusing solely on academic content

      C. Building upon students' cultural backgrounds and experiences

      D. Maintaining a neutral, objective stance

CHAPTER 2: ESTABLISHING A POSITIVE CLASSROOM

LESSON OBJECTIVE

At the end of this chapter, participants will be able to understand the following:

- Creating a welcoming and inclusive classroom culture
- Building positive relationships with students
- Promoting mutual respect and cooperation

CREATING A WELCOMING AND INCLUSIVE CLASSROOM CULTURE

Establishing a positive classroom culture is foundational to effective classroom management. Teachers must intentionally cultivate an environment that is welcoming, inclusive, and responsive to the diverse needs and backgrounds of all students.

This starts with ensuring the physical classroom space is clean, organized, and visually appealing. Displaying student work, incorporating culturally relevant materials and visuals, and arranging the furniture to facilitate collaboration can all contribute to an inviting atmosphere. Simple touches like plants, natural lighting, and student-created artwork can also make the space feel warm and nurturing.

Beyond the physical environment, teachers must focus on developing classroom norms, rituals, and procedures that promote a sense of community. This might involve co-creating a class mission statement, implementing daily check-ins or community circles, and establishing protocols for how students will interact with one another. When students have a voice in shaping these shared expectations, they are more likely to take ownership and adhere to them.

Importantly, building an inclusive culture also requires teachers to proactively address issues of bias, discrimination, and marginalization. They must be vigilant about identifying and interrupting microaggressions, stereotyping, and other exclusionary behaviors when they arise. By consistently modeling acceptance, empathy, and respect, teachers can foster a climate where all students feel valued and able to fully participate.

This might involve having open discussions about diversity, equity, and inclusion or incorporating culturally responsive teaching practices that validate and build upon students' backgrounds. Teachers should also be attuned to the unique needs and perspectives of underrepresented groups and make concerted efforts to ensure historically marginalized students feel heard and supported.

Ultimately, creating a welcoming and inclusive classroom culture is about more than just establishing rules and routines. It's about cultivating a genuine sense of community, belonging, and psychological safety—elements that are essential for students to take risks, collaborate, and thrive.

BUILDING POSITIVE RELATIONSHIPS WITH STUDENTS

At the heart of effective classroom management is the ability to build strong, caring relationships with students. When teachers demonstrate genuine interest, empathy, and concern for their students' wellbeing, it lays the foundation for productive interactions and mutual trust.

There are many strategies teachers can use to cultivate these positive relationships. Simple gestures like greeting students by name, learning about their interests and lives outside of school, and checking in on their emotional state can go a long way. Teachers should also make concerted efforts to have one-on-one conversations, provide personalized feedback, and celebrate student successes, big and small.

Importantly, building relationships must be reciprocal. Teachers should encourage students to share their lives, perspectives, and challenges. They should also be responsive to student needs and create opportunities for student voice and choice. By positioning themselves as collaborative partners in the learning process, teachers can foster a sense of belonging and shared investment.

When students feel truly seen, heard, and valued by their teacher, it cultivates a range of benefits. Students are more likely to be engaged, motivated, and self-directed in their learning. They're also more likely to feel comfortable taking academic risks, asking for help when needed, and persevering through challenges. Strong teacher-student relationships also enable more effective behavior management, as students are less likely to act out when there is mutual understanding and respect.

PROMOTING MUTUAL RESPECT AND COOPERATION

Classroom management is fundamentally about establishing an environment of mutual respect where teachers and students work together cooperatively toward shared goals. This requires teachers to model the behaviors and dispositions they want to see in their students.

For example, teachers should demonstrate patience, active listening, and a willingness to admit mistakes. They should also be clear and consistent in their communication of expectations while remaining flexible and open to student feedback. By treating students with dignity and fairness, teachers can inspire students to reciprocate that same respect.

Cultivating cooperation also involves giving students structured opportunities to collaborate. Through small group work, class discussions, and shared problem-solving, students can learn to communicate effectively, resolve conflicts, and support one another's learning. Teachers should provide clear guidelines and scaffolding to ensure these collaborative experiences are positive and productive.

When students see their teacher treating them with respect and creating space for their voices, it fosters a sense of empowerment and shared investment. In turn, students are more likely to take responsibility for their own behavior, listen to and support their peers, and engage meaningfully in the learning process. This cyclical dynamic of mutual respect and cooperation is essential for creating an orderly, productive classroom environment.

Ultimately, by creating a welcoming culture, building strong relationships, and promoting mutual respect, teachers can establish a classroom environment that is conducive to learning, growth, and success for all students.

QUIZ

1. Which of the following is NOT an important element of creating a welcoming and inclusive classroom environment?

    A. Displaying student work

    B. Incorporating culturally relevant materials

    C. Implementing strict behavior policies

    D. Arranging furniture to facilitate collaboration

2. What is the primary purpose of developing classroom norms, rituals, and procedures with student input?

    A. To establish teacher authority

    B. To promote student ownership and investment

    C. To minimize disruptions

    D. To create a sense of community

3. How can teachers proactively address issues of bias and discrimination in the classroom?

    A. By ignoring microaggressions and stereotyping

    B. By modeling acceptance, empathy, and respect

    C. By avoiding discussions about diversity and inclusion

    D. By treating all students equally regardless of background

4. What is one key benefit of teachers building strong, caring relationships with their students?

    A. It reduces the need for behavior management

    B. It increases student engagement and motivation

C. It improves academic achievement

D. All of the above

5. How can teachers promote mutual respect and cooperation in the classroom?

A. By establishing strict rules and consequences

B. By lecturing students on appropriate behavior

C. By providing structured opportunities for collaboration

D. By treating students with dignity and fairness

CHAPTER 3: DEVELOPING CLASSROOM RULES AND PROCEDURES

LESSON OBJECTIVE

At the end of this chapter, participants will be able to understand the following:

- Setting clear expectations and rules
- Teaching and reinforcing classroom procedures
- Addressing rule violations and consequences

SETTING CLEAR EXPECTATIONS AND RULES

One of the foundational elements of effective classroom management is establishing clear expectations and rules. When students understand exactly what is expected of them, it provides a sense of structure and predictability that supports on-task behavior and academic engagement.

Effective teachers invest time upfront to collaboratively develop a set of classroom norms and guidelines. This process should involve soliciting student input to ensure the rules feel relevant and meaningful. The resulting expectations should be framed in a positive way, focusing on what students should do rather than what they shouldn't.

For example, rather than a rule like "No talking during instruction," a more constructive expectation might be "Raise your hand and wait to be called on before speaking." This emphasizes the desired behavior (raising hands) rather than simply prohibiting an undesirable action.

It's also important that the number of classroom rules be limited to a manageable amount—typically, 5-7 rules maximum. This ensures students can easily remember and internalize the expectations. The rules should also be stated in clear, simple language that is developmentally appropriate for the grade level.

Once the classroom rules have been established, teachers must consistently reinforce them through visible displays, regular reminders, and specific positive feedback when students demonstrate the desired behaviors. This helps expectations become deeply ingrained in the classroom culture.

TEACHING AND REINFORCING CLASSROOM PROCEDURES

In addition to setting behavioral expectations, effective classroom management also involves teaching and reinforcing clear classroom procedures. These are the step-by-step routines that students follow for everyday tasks and transitions, such as:

- Entering and exiting the classroom
- Turning in and returning assignments
- Accessing classroom materials and technology
- Transitioning between activities
- Requesting permission or assistance

Just like with rules, these procedures should be explicitly taught, modeled, and practiced, especially at the start of the school year. Teachers can use strategies like role-playing, anchor charts, and gamification to help students internalize the expected behaviors.

Reinforcing these procedures consistently is key. When students demonstrate the desired actions, teachers should provide specific praise and positive reinforcement. If students struggle, teachers should reteach the procedure in a patient, non-punitive way. The goal is to help students automate the routines, so the classroom runs smoothly with minimal disruptions.

Importantly, classroom procedures should also be responsive to student needs and input. As the school year progresses, teachers should solicit feedback from students and be open to modifying procedures that aren't working as intended. By viewing procedures as dynamic rather than static, teachers can ensure they remain effective and relevant.

ADDRESSING RULE VIOLATIONS AND CONSEQUENCES

Despite proactive efforts to establish clear expectations, there will inevitably be times when students fail to meet the classroom rules and norms. How teachers respond in these situations is critical for maintaining order and trust.

Effective teachers approach rule violations with a calm, non-confrontational demeanor. They should avoid shaming or publicly calling out students and instead address the issue privately if possible. The focus should be on understanding the root cause of the misbehavior and guiding the student toward more constructive choices.

When consequences are necessary, they should be logical, fair, and consistently applied. This might involve temporarily removing a student from an activity, assigning a reflective writing task, or facilitating a restorative conversation. The goal is not to simply punish the student, but to help them learn from the experience and recommit to the classroom community.

Importantly, consequences should always be coupled with an opportunity for the student to "make amends" or demonstrate their willingness to improve. This could involve an apology, a commitment to following the rules moving forward, or some form of restitution. The aim is to repair the harm done and restore the student's sense of belonging.

In cases of more serious or persistent misbehavior, teachers may need to collaborate with school administration, counselors, and families to develop a comprehensive behavior intervention plan. This might entail implementing structured check-ins, providing additional support services, or creating a tailored system of reinforcements. The key is to take a proactive, solution-oriented approach rather than relying solely on punitive measures.

Ultimately, effective classroom management is not about rigid control or compliance. It's about striking the right balance between establishing clear parameters and empowering students to self-regulate and contribute to a positive learning community. By setting expectations, teaching procedures, and addressing violations thoughtfully, teachers can create an environment where students feel secure, motivated, and ready to learn.

QUIZ

1. What is the primary purpose of framing classroom rules in a positive way?
    - A. To be more authoritative
    - B. To emphasize desired behaviors
    - C. To simplify the rules
    - D. To avoid punishment

2. What is the recommended maximum number of classroom rules?
    - A. 3
    - B. 5
    - C. 7
    - D. 10

3. How can teachers reinforce classroom rules consistently?
    - A. By displaying the rules and providing regular reminders
    - B. By issuing consequences every time a rule is broken
    - C. By having students recite the rules daily
    - D. Both a and b

4. What is the primary purpose of explicitly teaching and practicing classroom procedures?
    - A. To automate routines and minimize disruptions
    - B. To give students a sense of control
    - C. To demonstrate the teacher's authority
    - D. Both a and b

5. What should be the focus when addressing rule violations, according to the content?

   A. Publicly shaming the student

   B. Issuing strict consequences

   C. Understanding the root cause and guiding the student

   D. Involving school administration

CHAPTER 4: EFFECTIVE LESSON PLANNING AND INSTRUCTION

LESSON OBJECTIVE

At the end of this chapter, participants will be able to understand the following:

- Designing engaging and well-structured lessons
- Incorporating different teaching strategies and techniques
- Managing transitions and maximizing instructional time

DESIGNING ENGAGING AND WELL-STRUCTURED LESSONS

Effective classroom management extends beyond just rules and procedures; it also encompasses the quality and delivery of instruction. When lessons are well-designed, engaging, and appropriately scaffolded, it significantly reduces the likelihood of disruptive behaviors.

At the outset, teachers should ensure their lesson plans have a clear, logical structure. This typically involves an opening to grab student attention, a focused instructional segment, opportunities for guided and independent practice, and a closing that reinforces key learning. Within this framework, teachers can incorporate a variety of instructional strategies to maintain student engagement.

For example, the opening of a lesson might utilize a short video, a thought-provoking question, or a creative hook to pique student curiosity. The instructional segment could then blend direct instruction with interactive elements like think-pair-shares, whiteboard responses, or student-led discussions. Opportunities for hands-on application, cooperative learning, and formative assessment should be strategically woven throughout.

Importantly, lesson design should also reflect an understanding of students' developmental needs, interests, and learning profiles. Teachers should differentiate content, process, and product to ensure all students can access the material and demonstrate their understanding. This might involve providing multi-modal resources, offering choice in how students engage, or scaffolding tasks for students working below grade level.

When lessons are meticulously planned, sequenced, and tailored to student needs, it creates an environment that is inherently more focused and productive. Students are less likely to get distracted or act out when they are immersed in meaningful, appropriately challenging learning experiences.

INCORPORATING DIFFERENT TEACHING STRATEGIES AND TECHNIQUES

In addition to intentional lesson design, effective classroom management also involves skillfully implementing a range of teaching strategies and techniques. By diversifying instructional approaches, teachers can better meet the varied learning preferences and needs of their students.

For example, direct instruction through modeling, explanation, and guided practice can be an important tool for teaching new concepts and skills. But it should be balanced with more active, student-centered approaches like project-based learning, Socratic seminars, and problem-solving activities. When students have opportunities to collaborate, inquire, and take an authentic role in the learning process, it cultivates higher levels of engagement and ownership.

Teachers should also leverage a repertoire of student engagement strategies, such as using attention-grabbing questions, incorporating multimedia, and providing opportunities for "brain breaks." Strategically pacing lessons to include a mix of passive and active learning experiences can help maintain student focus and energy levels.

Effective classroom managers also understand the value of clear, explicit communication. They ensure instructions and expectations are conveyed in a way that is accessible and unambiguous for all students. This might involve breaking down multi-step tasks, providing visual aids, and frequently checking for understanding.

Importantly, skilled teachers are also flexible and responsive in their instructional approach. They continuously monitor student reactions and adjust their plans on the fly to address emerging needs or challenges. This agility and in-the-moment decision-making are hallmarks of exemplary classroom management.

MANAGING TRANSITIONS AND MAXIMIZING INSTRUCTIONAL TIME

One of the critical responsibilities of classroom management is ensuring smooth, efficient transitions between lessons and activities. Poorly managed transitions can quickly lead to disruptions, off-task behavior, and lost instructional time.

Effective teachers have clear, well-rehearsed procedures in place for common classroom transitions, such as entering the room, shifting between whole-class and small-group work, and preparing to dismiss. They utilize strategies like countdowns, timers, and nonverbal cues to signal when it's time to shift gears. Students are actively involved in these routines, taking ownership of their role in making transitions seamless.

Beyond just managing transitions, skilled classroom managers also work relentlessly to maximize the time devoted to high-quality instruction and learning. They minimize disruptions, streamline administrative tasks, and maintain a brisk, focused pace throughout lessons. For example, they may have students turn in assignments as they enter the room, distribute materials ahead of time, or leverage technology to speed up certain procedures.

Importantly, effective teachers also recognize the value of strategic pacing and "wait time" within their lessons. They intersperse periods of direct instruction with opportunities for processing, practice, and movement. By giving students regular brain breaks and chances to interact, they help sustain attention and cognitive engagement.

Ultimately, masterful classroom management is about more than just enforcing rules; it's about orchestrating a learning environment that is structured, efficient, and responsive to students' instructional needs. When teachers design lessons thoughtfully, employ a diverse repertoire of teaching techniques, and skillfully manage transitions and time, it creates the conditions for meaningful learning to occur.

QUIZ

1. What is the primary purpose of ensuring lessons have a clear, logical structure?

    A. To maintain the teacher's authority

    B. To reduce the likelihood of disruptive behaviors

    C. To increase the rigor of the instruction

    D. To cover more content in less time

2. How can teachers incorporate interactive elements into the instructional segment of a lesson?

    A. By using think-pair-share activities

    B. By having students lead discussions

    C. By incorporating whiteboard responses

    D. All of the above

3. What is the primary purpose of differentiating lesson content, process, and product?

    A. To challenge advanced students

    B. To maximize instructional efficiency

    C. To meet the diverse needs of all students

    D. To increase teacher control

4. Which of the following is an example of a student engagement strategy teachers can leverage?

    A. Providing opportunities for "brain breaks"

    B. Delivering lengthy lectures

C. Assigning independent seatwork

   D. Both a and b

5. What is the primary purpose of having well-rehearsed transition procedures in place?

   A. To demonstrate the teacher's authority

   B. To minimize disruptions and lost instructional time

   C. To create a sense of predictability for students

   D. Both b and c

CHAPTER 5: MANAGING STUDENT BEHAVIOR

LESSON OBJECTIVE

At the end of this chapter, participants will be able to understand the following:

- Identifying and addressing challenging behaviors
- Implementing proactive strategies for behavior management
- Using positive reinforcement and effective discipline techniques

IDENTIFYING AND ADDRESSING CHALLENGING BEHAVIORS

Even in the most well-managed classrooms, teachers will encounter student behaviors that disrupt the learning environment. The ability to accurately identify the root causes of these challenges and respond appropriately is a key aspect of effective classroom management.

Some common types of disruptive behaviors teachers may encounter include:

- ❖ Defiance and noncompliance
- ❖ Disengagement and off-task actions
- ❖ Aggressive or violent outbursts
- ❖ Excessive talking or disrupting others
- ❖ Inappropriate language or actions

When dealing with these types of behaviors, it's important for teachers to take a thoughtful, objective approach. They should aim to understand the underlying reasons driving the student's actions, which may include factors like unmet academic or social-emotional needs, trauma, or mental health challenges.

By taking the time to observe patterns, collect data, and have empathetic conversations, teachers can develop a more comprehensive understanding of what's really going on. This allows them to craft nuanced interventions that address the true source of the behavior, rather than just trying to control the outward symptoms.

For example, a student who is constantly blurting out or refusing to follow directions may be struggling with impulse control due to ADHD or a history of adversity. Addressing this could involve working with the student to develop self-regulation strategies, providing sensory supports, and collaborating with families and school support staff.

Importantly, responding to challenging behaviors should always be approached through a culturally responsive and trauma-informed lens. Teachers must be attuned to how factors like race, socioeconomic status, and disability may shape a student's experiences and behaviors. Disciplinary responses that are overly punitive or fail to account for student needs can actually exacerbate problems and damage teacher-student relationships.

IMPLEMENTING PROACTIVE STRATEGIES FOR BEHAVIOR MANAGEMENT

While effectively addressing in-the-moment disruptions is crucial, the most skilled classroom managers also focus heavily on proactive strategies to prevent behavioral issues from arising in the first place. This involves intentionally structuring the classroom environment, teaching social-emotional skills, and fostering a positive, supportive climate.

As discussed earlier, establishing clear expectations, teaching routines, and utilizing engaging instructional practices are all essential proactive measures. Beyond that, teachers should also:

❖ Cultivate strong, supportive relationships with all students.
❖ Teach and reinforce social-emotional competencies like self-regulation.
❖ Provide sensory and movement breaks and other accommodations as needed.
❖ Develop individualized behavior intervention plans for high-needs students.
❖ Collaborate with families, counselors, and other support staff.

When teachers are attuned to the unique needs and triggers of individual students, they can put preventative systems in place to avoid escalations. For example, they may give a student a designated "calm down" area, arrange seating to minimize distractions, or have a pre-arranged signal to redirect off-task behavior.

The goal is to create a classroom where minor misbehaviors are quickly and gently redirected, allowing learning to continue with minimal disruption. By prioritizing proactive, relationship-centered strategies, teachers can dramatically reduce the frequency and intensity of challenging behaviors.

USING POSITIVE REINFORCEMENT AND EFFECTIVE DISCIPLINE TECHNIQUES

When addressing behavioral issues, effective classroom managers rely heavily on positive reinforcement strategies rather than purely punitive consequences. The underlying philosophy is that students are more likely to repeat desirable behaviors when they are positively recognized and rewarded.

Reinforcement can take many forms, such as verbal praise, tangible rewards, or special privileges. The key is to identify what motivates each individual student and provide reinforcement immediately following the target behavior. Over time, this helps shape and maintain the desired behavior.

That said, there are certainly times when disciplinary consequences are necessary, particularly for more serious rule violations. However, skilled teachers utilize a range of discipline techniques that go beyond simply issuing punishments. These may include:

- Logical consequences (*e.g.*, losing privileges related to the misbehavior)
- Restorative practices (*e.g.*, having the student make amends)
- Reflective activities (*e.g.*, having the student complete a think sheet)
- Behavior contracts or intervention plans
- Collaborating with families and school support staff

The overall goal is to help students develop self-awareness, self-regulation, and a sense of personal responsibility. Consequences should be delivered calmly, consistently, and with an emphasis on problem-solving and future improvement, not just compliance.

Ultimately, effective behavior management is about striking the right balance between proactive, preventative strategies and responsive, restorative interventions. When teachers prioritize building strong relationships, teaching social-emotional skills, and reinforcing positive behaviors, it lays the groundwork for an orderly, productive classroom where all students can thrive.

QUIZ

1. What is the primary purpose of ensuring lessons have a clear, logical structure?

    A. To maintain the teacher's authority

    B. To reduce the likelihood of disruptive behaviors

    C. To increase the rigor of the instruction

    D. To cover more content in less time

2. How can teachers incorporate interactive elements into the instructional segment of a lesson?

    A. By using think-pair-share activities

    B. By having students lead discussions

    C. By incorporating whiteboard responses

    D. All of the above

3. What is the primary purpose of differentiating lesson content, process, and product?

    A. To challenge advanced students

    B. To maximize instructional efficiency

    C. To meet the diverse needs of all students

    D. To increase teacher control

4. Which of the following is an example of a student engagement strategy teachers can leverage?

    A. Providing opportunities for "brain breaks"

    B. Delivering lengthy lectures

C. Assigning independent seatwork

D. Both a and b

5. What is the primary purpose of having well-rehearsed transition procedures in place?

    A. To demonstrate the teacher's authority

    B. To minimize disruptions and lost instructional time

    C. To create a sense of predictability for students

    D. Both b and c

CHAPTER 6: PROMOTING STUDENT ENGAGEMENT AND PARTICIPATION

LESSON OBJECTIVE

At the end of this chapter, participants will be able to understand the following:

- Creating a stimulating learning environment
- Encouraging active learning and student involvement
- Differentiating instruction to meet diverse student needs

CREATING A STIMULATING LEARNING ENVIRONMENT

Beyond just establishing routines and managing behavior, effective classroom management also involves cultivating a physical and social environment that is stimulating, engaging, and conducive to learning. This requires teachers to thoughtfully design the classroom space and foster an overall tone of excitement and discovery.

From an environmental standpoint, teachers should strive to create a visually interesting and multi-sensory classroom. This might involve displaying student work, incorporating natural elements like plants, and strategically arranging furniture to facilitate collaboration and movement. Utilizing colorful, high-quality instructional materials and educational technology can also contribute to an energetic, vibrant atmosphere.

Importantly, the physical environment should also be responsive to student needs and learning preferences. For example, providing a variety of flexible seating options (*e.g.*, standing desks, bean bags, exercise balls) allows students to choose the setup that helps them focus best. Having clearly defined spaces for individual work, small group discussion, and hands-on exploration further supports differentiated learning.

Beyond the physical elements, skilled classroom managers also cultivate a social-emotional climate that is warm, supportive, and intellectually stimulating. They model enthusiasm for the content, encourage students to take intellectual risks, and celebrate both effort and achievement. This helps foster a growth mindset where students feel safe to make mistakes and push themselves.

Teachers can also incorporate rituals, traditions, and opportunities for student voice that reinforce a sense of community and shared purpose within the classroom. Simple practices like morning meetings, student-led presentations, and class celebrations can go a long way in building a vibrant, collaborative learning culture.

Ultimately, creating a stimulating learning environment is about more than just aesthetics; it's about intentionally shaping a space that sparks curiosity, engagement, and a joy of learning. When students feel energized, valued, and eager to participate, it sets the stage for meaningful academic and social-emotional growth.

ENCOURAGING ACTIVE LEARNING AND STUDENT INVOLVEMENT

While a visually appealing, well-structured classroom is important, effective classroom management also requires teachers to actively engage students in the learning process. Passive, teacher-centered approaches tend to breed boredom and disruptive behaviors, while active learning strategies keep students mentally and physically invested.

Skilled teachers use a variety of techniques to promote active student involvement, such as:

- Posing thought-provoking questions that encourage discussion and critical thinking
- incorporating opportunities for hands-on experimentation, project-based learning, and real-world application
- Utilizing collaborative learning structures like think-pair-share, jigsaw activities, and group problem-solving
- Empowering students to take ownership of their learning through student-led inquiry and presentations

When students are actively participating, constructing knowledge, and applying skills, it enhances their engagement, retention, and overall academic performance. Moreover, active learning strategies provide natural outlets for students' physical and social energy, reducing the likelihood of disruptive behaviors.

Importantly, active learning should be balanced with more direct instruction, modeling, and guided practice, as appropriate. The key is to create a healthy blend of teacher-led and student-centered activities that address diverse learning needs and preferences. With the right scaffolding and support, even complex content can be explored through active, hands-on approaches.

DIFFERENTIATING INSTRUCTION TO MEET DIVERSE STUDENT NEEDS

Underlying all of the classroom management strategies discussed thus far is a fundamental commitment to differentiating instruction. Effective teachers understand that students come to the classroom with a wide range of backgrounds, interests, learning profiles, and readiness levels. Cookie-cutter, one-size-fits-all approaches simply won't work.

Instead, skilled classroom managers employ a range of differentiation strategies to ensure all students can access and engage with the curriculum. This may involve providing scaffolded supports, offering student choice, or utilizing flexible grouping structures. For example, a teacher might give some students access to audiobooks or text-to-speech tools, allow others to demonstrate their learning through an alternate project, and group students strategically for collaborative tasks.

Importantly, differentiation is not just about modifying the content or product; it's also about varying the instructional process and learning environment. This could mean incorporating movement breaks for students who need sensory input, creating quiet work zones for those who thrive in more solitary settings, or leveraging technology to personalize the learning experience.

Beyond just addressing academic differences, effective classroom managers also strive to be responsive to the diverse social, emotional, and cultural needs of their students. This might involve implementing universal screening, providing access to counseling services, or using culturally responsive teaching practices that validate and build upon students' backgrounds.

Ultimately, a "one-size-fits-all" approach to classroom management simply doesn't work. By instead embracing the diversity of their students and differentiating accordingly, teachers can create an environment where all learners can flourish. This requires flexibility, creativity, and a deep understanding of child development, but the payoff is a thriving, inclusive classroom community.

QUIZ

1. What is an essential aspect of effective classroom management besides establishing routines and managing behavior?

    A. Creating a stimulating learning environment

    B. Maintaining a strict discipline policy

    C. Ignoring the physical environment

    D. Focusing solely on direct instruction

2. How can teachers create a visually interesting and multi-sensory classroom?

    A. By avoiding the display of student work

    B. By incorporating natural elements like plants

    C. By minimizing collaboration and movement

    D. By using only black and white instructional materials

3. What is an example of a differentiation strategy mentioned in the text?

    A. Providing the same learning materials for all students

    B. Offering only one instructional approach

    C. Utilizing flexible grouping structures

    D. Ignoring students' diverse backgrounds and interests

4. What are some techniques teachers use to promote active student involvement?

    A. Encouraging passive learning approaches

    B. Asking closed-ended questions

    C. Incorporating hands-on experimentation

    D. Avoiding collaborative learning structures

5. Why is differentiation important in classroom management?

        A. It simplifies the teaching process for educators

        B. It ensures that all students learn at the same pace

        C. It acknowledges and addresses diverse student needs

        D. It limits access to learning resources

CHAPTER 7: CLASSROOM ORGANIZATION AND MATERIALS MANAGEMENT

LESSON OBJECTIVE

At the end of this chapter, participants will be able to understand the following:

- Arranging the physical space for optimal learning
- Managing classroom resources and materials
- Utilizing technology effectively in the classroom

ARRANGING THE PHYSICAL SPACE FOR OPTIMAL LEARNING

The physical arrangement of the classroom can have a powerful impact on student behavior, engagement, and overall learning. Effective classroom managers thoughtfully design the space to support their instructional goals and meet the diverse needs of their students.

A well-organized classroom typically has clearly defined areas for different activities, such as a whole-group meeting area, individual workspaces, small group collaboration zones, and hands-on exploration stations. This helps students understand the expected behaviors and routines associated with each space.

Furniture and equipment should be arranged to maximize sightlines and minimize distractions. Desks or tables might be grouped in clusters to facilitate discussion and teamwork while also allowing the teacher to easily circulate and provide support. Bookshelves, storage units, and other larger pieces should be positioned strategically to divide the room into logical sections without creating blind spots or crowded walkways.

Importantly, the classroom layout should also be responsive to students' learning needs and preferences. For example, providing flexible seating options like yoga balls, beanbags, and standing desks allows students to choose the setup that helps them focus best. Having a dedicated "calm down" or sensory area can also be beneficial for students who need to re-regulate during the school day.

Beyond the core furnishings, teachers should also thoughtfully curate the visual elements of the space. Strategically displaying student work, anchor charts, and educational posters can reinforce learning objectives and cultivate a sense of pride and ownership. Incorporating natural elements like plants, soft lighting, and inspiring artwork can also contribute to a warm, welcoming ambiance.

Ultimately, the physical classroom environment should be designed as a dynamic, supportive tool for learning, not just a static backdrop. When teachers put careful thought into the arrangement and aesthetics of the space, it can have a profound impact on student behavior, focus, and academic achievement.

MANAGING CLASSROOM RESOURCES AND MATERIALS

Effective classroom management also involves the thoughtful organization and distribution of resources, supplies, and instructional materials. When these tangible elements of the learning environment are well managed, it minimizes disruptions, promotes student independence, and maximizes instructional time.

To start, teachers should have a system for storing, accessing, and replenishing classroom materials. This might involve labeled storage bins, color-coded organization systems, and designated student supply areas. Clear, consistent procedures should be established for how students retrieve, use, and return items throughout the day.

Instructional resources like textbooks, library books, technology devices, and hands-on manipulatives should also be carefully inventoried, maintained, and distributed. By implementing efficient checkout systems, establishing clear expectations, and training students on proper care and usage, teachers can ensure these valuable learning tools are utilized effectively.

Importantly, the management of classroom resources should empower students to take ownership and become more self-directed in their learning. For example, having students retrieve their own materials, restock supplies, and even participate in inventory audits can foster a greater sense of responsibility and investment.

When physical resources are organized, accessible, and used purposefully, they contribute to an overall classroom environment that is structured, efficient, and conducive to learning. Students are less likely to get distracted or waste time searching for materials, and teachers can focus their energy on delivering high-quality instruction.

UTILIZING TECHNOLOGY EFFECTIVELY IN THE CLASSROOM

In today's digitally driven world, the skillful integration of educational technology is an increasingly important aspect of effective classroom management. When used strategically, technology can enhance student engagement, differentiate instruction, and streamline administrative tasks.

Skilled teachers carefully select and implement technology tools that align with their curricular objectives and complement their pedagogical approach. This might involve using interactive whiteboards, student response systems, or online learning platforms to deliver content, facilitate activities, and assess learning.

Importantly, the integration of technology should not be an end in itself but rather a means to an end—enhancing the teaching and learning process. Effective classroom managers understand that technology is most powerful when it is seamlessly woven into lessons rather than used as a standalone add-on.

They also prioritize establishing clear procedures and expectations for how students will access, use, and maintain technology in the classroom. This might involve teaching digital citizenship skills, implementing device management systems, and addressing any equity issues related to technology access.

Additionally, skilled teachers recognize that the integration of technology requires ongoing professional development and troubleshooting. They remain flexible and adaptable, constantly evaluating the efficacy of their tech-enabled strategies and making adjustments as needed. This allows them to continuously leverage the power of technology to foster engagement, differentiation, and efficiency in their classrooms.

Ultimately, the physical design of the classroom, the management of resources, and the integration of technology are all critical elements of effective classroom management. When teachers thoughtfully orchestrate these tangible aspects of the learning environment, it lays the groundwork for an orderly, productive, and enriching educational experience for all students.

QUIZ

1. How does the physical arrangement of the classroom impact student behavior and learning?

    A. It has no impact on student behavior

    B. It minimizes distractions and promotes focus

    C. It increases disruptions and decreases focus

    D. It only affects the teacher's ability to circulate the room

2. What are some examples of areas that should be clearly defined in a well-organized classroom?

    A. Only a whole-group meeting area

    B. Only individual workspaces

    C. Whole-group meeting area, individual workspaces, small group collaboration zones, and hands-on exploration stations

    D. Only small group collaboration zones

3. How can teachers empower students to take ownership of classroom resources?

    A. By hoarding all materials and supplies

    B. By establishing clear procedures and expectations for material usage

    C. By keeping materials inaccessible to students

    D. By not allowing students to participate in inventory audits

4. What is an important consideration when integrating technology into the classroom?

    A. Using technology as a standalone add-on

    B. Prioritizing digital citizenship skills

    C. Avoiding ongoing professional development

    D. Not addressing equity issues related to technology access

5. What is the overarching goal of effective classroom management regarding technology integration?

    A. Using technology as the primary means of instruction

    B. Making technology the focus of every lesson

    C. Enhancing teaching and learning through strategic technology use

    D. Avoiding technology use altogether

CHAPTER 8: EFFECTIVE COMMUNICATION AND COLLABORATION

LESSON OBJECTIVE

At the end of this chapter, participants will be able to understand the following:

- Establishing open lines of communication with students and parents
- Fostering a collaborative classroom community
- Resolving conflicts and addressing concerns

ESTABLISHING OPEN LINES OF COMMUNICATION WITH STUDENTS AND PARENTS

Effective classroom management extends well beyond the four walls of the classroom. It also requires teachers to cultivate strong communication channels with their students' families and caregivers.

When teachers establish positive, trust-based relationships with parents and guardians, it benefits students in numerous ways. First, it allows for the open exchange of information about a child's academic progress, social-emotional development, and any challenges or concerns that may be impacting their learning. This holistic understanding can then inform more targeted and effective interventions.

Additionally, regular communication helps parents feel more empowered to support their child's success at home. Teachers can provide practical tips and resources for reinforcing classroom expectations, supporting homework, and encouraging positive behavior. This bridges the gap between home and school, creating a unified front that benefits the whole child.

Importantly, communication should be proactive, personalized, and two-way. Teachers should initiate regular check-ins, whether through conferences, phone calls, or digital platforms, and actively listen to parents' perspectives and concerns. They should also be responsive in addressing any issues that arise, working collaboratively to find solutions.

Beyond just connecting with parents, effective classroom managers also prioritize fostering open communication with their students. They create structured opportunities for dialogue, such as morning meetings, one-on-one conferences, and class discussions. This allows them to better understand students' interests, needs, and challenges and make adjustments to support their learning.

Importantly, teachers should model the communication skills they hope to see from their students. This means actively listening, validating emotions, and responding with empathy and respect. By cultivating a classroom culture of transparent, solution-focused communication, teachers can empower students to become self-advocates and engaged partners in their own academic and social-emotional growth.

FOSTERING A COLLABORATIVE CLASSROOM COMMUNITY

Classroom management is not just about establishing rules and procedures; it's also about cultivating a genuine sense of community, belonging, and shared investment among students. When teachers intentionally foster collaboration and collective responsibility, it dramatically reduces discipline issues and creates an environment conducive to learning.

This begins with teachers modeling and explicitly teaching important social-emotional skills like active listening, perspective-taking, conflict resolution, and teamwork. Students should have frequent opportunities to engage in structured cooperative learning activities where they must work interdependently to accomplish shared goals.

Teachers can also involve students in the co-creation of classroom norms, rituals, and shared spaces. By giving students, a voice in shaping the learning environment, they develop a greater sense of ownership and commitment to upholding those community standards.

Fostering a collaborative classroom culture also means celebrating individual and collective achievements and responding to misbehavior through a restorative, community-focused lens. When students feel valued, empowered, and mutually accountable, they are less likely to engage in disruptive behaviors that undermine the common good.

Ultimately, an effectively managed classroom is one where students see themselves as partners, not just passive recipients, in the learning process. By cultivating a spirit of collaboration, teachers can leverage the power of peer influence and shared responsibility to create a thriving, productive learning environment.

RESOLVING CONFLICTS AND ADDRESSING CONCERNS

Even in the most well-managed classrooms, conflicts and challenges will inevitably arise. Skilled classroom managers have a toolbox of strategies for resolving interpersonal issues and addressing concerns in a proactive, solution-oriented manner.

When dealing with student-to-student conflicts, teachers should first aim to de-escalate the situation by separating the involved parties, remaining calm, and avoiding accusatory language. They can then facilitate a restorative conversation, guiding the students through a structured process of taking responsibility, expressing remorse, and identifying ways to make amends.

For more serious behavioral incidents or persistent problems, teachers should document the issue carefully and collaborate with school administrators, counselors, and families to develop a comprehensive intervention plan. This might involve conducting functional behavior assessments, implementing behavior contracts, or connecting students with specialized support services.

Importantly, teachers must also be attentive to and responsive when students express concerns about issues like bullying, discrimination, or feeling unsafe. They should take all such reports seriously, investigate thoroughly, and enact appropriate consequences and corrective actions. Cultivating an environment where students feel empowered to speak up is essential for maintaining a positive, inclusive classroom culture.

However, conflict resolution and concern-addressing aren't just about dealing with student-related issues. Effective classroom managers also prioritize proactive, solutions-focused communication with parents and caregivers. When concerns or disagreements arise, they approach them with empathy, professionalism, and a genuine commitment to finding a mutually agreeable path forward.

Ultimately, skilled classroom managers understand that conflict and challenges are a natural part of the educational process. By having a well-developed repertoire of conflict resolution strategies and by fostering a collaborative, communicative classroom community, teachers can navigate these issues constructively and maintain an environment conducive to learning and growth for all.

QUIZ

1. What are the benefits of establishing positive communication channels with parents and guardians?

    A. It increases student independence.

    B. It reduces the need for classroom rules.

    C. It allows for open exchange of information about a child's progress.

    D. It decreases student engagement.

2. How can teachers foster open communication with students?

    A. By avoiding structured opportunities for dialogue

    B. By modeling good communication skills

    C. By limiting interactions to disciplinary matters only

    D. By disregarding students' interests and challenges

3. What is essential for fostering a collaborative classroom community?

    A. Maintaining strict disciplinary procedures

    B. Celebrating individual achievements only

    C. Involving students in the co-creation of classroom norms

    D. Avoiding conflict resolution strategies

4. How should teachers address conflicts between students?

    A. By escalating the situation immediately

    B. By facilitating a restorative conversation

    C. By ignoring the conflict

D. By blaming one party without investigation

5. Why is proactive communication with parents and caregivers important?

A. It creates more conflicts in the classroom.

B. It minimizes the need for collaboration.

C. It helps address concerns and disagreements constructively.

D. It increases student independence.

CHAPTER 9: BUILDING EFFECTIVE CLASSROOM ROUTINES

LESSON OBJECTIVE

At the end of this chapter, participants will be able to understand the following:

- Establishing consistent daily routines and procedures
- Managing transitions and disruptions
- Promoting student independence and responsibility:

ESTABLISHING CONSISTENT DAILY ROUTINES AND PROCEDURES

One of the foundational elements of effective classroom management is the implementation of consistent daily routines and procedures. When students know exactly what to expect and how to operate within the classroom, it provides a sense of structure, stability, and predictability that supports on-task behavior and academic engagement.

Effective teachers invest significant time at the beginning of the school year to collaboratively develop and communicate clear classroom norms, rules, and protocols. This might include procedures for entering and exiting the room, turning in assignments, accessing materials and technology, and transitioning between activities.

These routines should be reinforced through visible displays, verbal reminders, and specific positive feedback when students demonstrate the expected actions. Over time, the goal is for these procedures to become so deeply ingrained that they become almost automatic for students.

Importantly, daily routines should also be responsive to student needs and feedback. As the school year progresses, teachers should solicit input from students and be open to refining or modifying procedures that aren't working as intended. By viewing routines as dynamic rather than static, teachers can ensure they remain relevant, efficient, and supportive of learning.

Establishing consistent routines doesn't mean the classroom has to feel rigid or overly controlled, however. Skilled classroom managers know how to balance structure with flexibility, incorporating opportunities for student choice and creativity within the predictable flow of the day. The key is creating an environment that feels orderly and secure while also being intellectually stimulating and engaging.

MANAGING TRANSITIONS AND DISRUPTIONS

In addition to daily routines, effective classroom management also requires teachers to skillfully navigate the numerous transitions and potential disruptions that arise throughout a typical school day. Poorly managed transitions can quickly lead to off-task behavior, lost instructional time, and classroom chaos.

Exemplary classroom managers have clear, well-rehearsed procedures in place for common classroom transitions, such as entering the room, shifting between whole-class and small-group work, and preparing to dismiss. They utilize strategies like countdowns, timers, and nonverbal cues to signal when it's time to shift gears.

Students are actively involved in these routines, taking ownership of their role in making transitions seamless.

Beyond just managing transitions, skilled classroom managers also work tirelessly to minimize disruptions and maintain a brisk, focused pace throughout lessons. They may have students turn in assignments as they enter the room, distribute materials ahead of time, or leverage technology to speed up certain administrative tasks. This allows them to devote more time to high-quality instruction and learning.

Importantly, effective teachers also recognize the value of strategic pacing and "wait time" within their lessons. They intersperse periods of direct instruction with opportunities for processing, practice, and movement. By giving students regular brain breaks and chances to interact, they help sustain attention and cognitive engagement.

When inevitable disruptions do occur, whether from technology issues, outside announcements, or student misbehavior, skilled classroom managers respond quickly and calmly to refocus the class. They have a repertoire of redirection techniques at their disposal, from simple eye contact and proximity control to explicitly re-stating expectations to temporarily separating a disruptive student. The goal is to address the issue swiftly and unobtrusively, minimizing the impact on instructional time.

PROMOTING STUDENT INDEPENDENCE AND RESPONSIBILITY

Effective classroom management is ultimately not just about teachers imposing order and control; it's also about cultivating student self-regulation, independence, and a sense of shared responsibility for the learning environment.

Skilled teachers intentionally teach, model, and reinforce important self-management skills, such as time management, organization, and problem-solving. They create structures that empower students to take an active role in classroom routines and procedures, whether it's distributing materials, tracking their own progress, or enforcing community norms.

By gradually releasing more autonomy and decision-making to students, teachers help them develop the metacognitive awareness and executive functioning skills that are essential for long-term success. Students who feel a sense of ownership and agency within the classroom are more likely to be engaged, motivated learners who internalize positive behavioral habits.

Importantly, promoting student independence doesn't mean abandoning all structure and support. Effective classroom managers know how to carefully scaffold self-directed learning, providing the right balance of freedom and guidance based on students' developmental needs and capabilities. They also maintain an awareness of when to intervene and re-establish teacher-directed routines if students struggle to self-regulate.

Ultimately, the most skilled classroom managers understand that their role is not just to control student behavior but to empower students to become self-directed, responsible citizens of the classroom community. By establishing consistent routines, managing transitions seamlessly, and gradually instilling a sense of independence, they create an environment that fosters sustainable learning, engagement, and social-emotional growth.

QUIZ

1. Why are consistent daily routines and procedures important in effective classroom management?

    A. They create chaos and confusion.

    B. They minimize predictability for students.

    C. They provide a sense of structure and stability.

    D. They are unnecessary for student learning.

2. What strategies can teachers use to manage transitions effectively?

    A. Avoiding transitions altogether

    B. Utilizing countdowns, timers, and nonverbal cues

    C. Ignoring transitions and letting students figure it out

    D. Allowing disruptions during transitions

3. How do skilled classroom managers respond to disruptions during lessons?

    A. They panic and lose control of the class.

    B. They respond quickly and calmly to refocus the class.

    C. They ignore disruptions and continue teaching.

    D. They blame students for disruptions.

4. What is the goal of promoting student independence and responsibility in the classroom?

    A. To maintain strict control over students

    B. To foster a sense of dependency on the teacher

    C. To cultivate self-regulation and agency in students

D. To discourage students from taking ownership of their learning

5. How do effective teachers balance structure and flexibility in the classroom?

    A. By imposing rigid rules with no room for student choice

    B. By completely abandoning all classroom routines

    C. By incorporating opportunities for student choice and creativity within consistent routines

    D. By ignoring students' needs and preferences

CHAPTER 10: REFLECTING AND GROWING AS A CLASSROOM MANAGER

LESSON OBJECTIVE

At the end of this chapter, participants will be able to understand the following:

- Reflecting on teaching practices and classroom management strategies
- Seeking feedback and professional development opportunities
- Developing a personal action plan for continuous improvement

REFLECTING ON TEACHING PRACTICES AND CLASSROOM MANAGEMENT STRATEGIES

Effective classroom management is not a static set of techniques that can be rigidly applied. Rather, it is a dynamic, nuanced skill that requires ongoing reflection, refinement, and adaptation. The most skilled classroom managers are those who consistently examine the impact of their practices, solicit feedback, and make intentional adjustments to better meet the needs of their students.

Self-reflection should be a regular part of a teacher's practice. After each lesson or school day, they should take time to critically analyze what worked well, what challenges arose, and how they responded. Key questions to consider might include:

❖ Were my instructional strategies effective in engaging students and supporting learning?

❖ How well did my classroom routines and procedures function, and where are there opportunities for improvement?

- ❖ How did I handle disruptive behaviors or difficult transitions, and is there a more effective approach I could have taken?
- ❖ To what extent was I able to differentiate instruction and support the diverse needs of my students?
- ❖ Where did I observe positive student-teacher and student-student interactions, and how can I build upon those?

By systematically reflecting on their own decision-making and the resulting student outcomes, teachers can identify areas of strength as well as aspects of their practice that require refinement. This self-awareness is essential for developing more nuanced classroom management skills over time.

SEEKING FEEDBACK AND PROFESSIONAL DEVELOPMENT OPPORTUNITIES

Of course, self-reflection alone is not enough. Effective classroom managers also proactively seek out feedback and support from a variety of sources to further inform and enhance their practice.

This might involve soliciting input from students through anonymous surveys or class discussions. Students can provide invaluable insights into what instructional approaches resonate with them, what classroom routines are working well, and where they feel their needs are not being met. Teachers should approach this feedback with an open mindset, carefully considering how to incorporate student voice.

Seeking feedback from colleagues, instructional coaches, and school administrators can also be immensely helpful. Observing other teachers, participating in peer coaching, and engaging in collaborative problem-solving can all uncover new strategies and perspectives. Administrators can provide important school-level context, offer constructive feedback, and connect teachers with relevant professional development opportunities.

Speaking of professional development, continually expanding one's knowledge and skills is essential for effective classroom management. Teachers should actively seek out workshops, courses, and online resources that address areas they have identified for growth, whether it's implementing restorative practices, differentiating instruction, or cultivating student self-regulation.

Importantly, professional development should not be viewed as a one-time event but rather as an ongoing commitment to lifelong learning. Teachers should regularly assess their own needs, stay attuned to emerging best practices in the field, and be open to experimenting with new approaches in their classrooms.

DEVELOPING A PERSONAL ACTION PLAN FOR CONTINUOUS IMPROVEMENT

By consistently reflecting on their practice, seeking feedback, and engaging in professional development, teachers can develop a clear understanding of their classroom management strengths and areas for growth. The final step is to translate these insights into a personalized action plan for continuous improvement.

This plan should identify specific, measurable goals the teacher wants to achieve, along with the concrete steps they will take to reach those objectives. For example, a teacher might set a goal of improving their use of positive reinforcement strategies and outline action steps like researching effective reinforcement techniques, modeling them in their lessons, and tracking student responses.

The action plan should also include mechanisms for self-monitoring and accountability. This might involve setting milestones or deadlines, enlisting the support of a coach or mentor, and regularly revisiting and revising the plan as needed.

Importantly, an effective action plan is not a static document but rather a living, breathing tool that evolves alongside the teacher's practice. As they implement new strategies, gather feedback, and refine their approach, the plan should be updated to reflect their growth and emerging priorities.

By embracing this cyclical process of reflection, feedback, professional development, and goal-setting, teachers can ensure their classroom management skills remain sharp, responsive, and continuously improving. It is this dedication to ongoing growth and refinement that distinguishes the most exemplary classroom managers.

Ultimately, effective classroom management is not about perfection or a one-size-fits-all approach. Rather, it is a dynamic, complex practice that requires constant learning, adaptation, and a genuine commitment to meeting the diverse needs of all students. By engaging in this reflective, iterative process, teachers can create learning environments that are structured, engaging, and conducive to meaningful, joyful educational experiences.

QUIZ

1. Why is self-reflection important for effective classroom management?
    - A. It allows teachers to criticize their students
    - B. It helps teachers identify areas of strength and areas for improvement
    - C. It encourages teachers to avoid seeking feedback
    - D. It only focuses on what went wrong in the classroom

2. What are some sources from which teachers can seek feedback to enhance their classroom management?
    - A. Students, colleagues, and school administrators
    - B. Only school administrators
    - C. Only colleagues
    - D. None, as self-reflection is sufficient

3. What is the purpose of professional development for teachers?
    - A. To avoid seeking feedback
    - B. To enhance classroom management skills
    - C. To criticize students
    - D. To demonstrate perfection in teaching

4. What should be included in a teacher's action plan for continuous improvement?
    - A. Specific, measurable goals and concrete steps to achieve them
    - B. Vague goals with no actionable steps

C. No plan is necessary for improvement

D. Goals unrelated to classroom management

5. Why is the process of reflection, feedback, professional development, and goal-setting considered cyclical?

   A. Because it only happens once a year
   B. Because it happens repeatedly over time
   C. Because it is not necessary for effective classroom management
   D. Because it involves rigid, unchanging practices

CONCLUSION

In conclusion, effective classroom management is the foundation upon which all great teaching and learning are built. By establishing clear expectations, fostering positive relationships, and crafting engaging, well-structured lessons, teachers can create learning environments that are orderly, inclusive, and conducive to student success.

Skillful classroom managers are not just disciplinarians; they are skilled architects who thoughtfully design every aspect of the classroom experience. From the physical layout to the daily routines, from the selection of instructional strategies to the management of resources, each element is carefully orchestrated to maximize engagement, minimize disruptions, and empower students to take an active role in their own growth.

Ultimately, mastering the art of classroom management requires an ongoing commitment to reflection, feedback, and professional growth. By continuously assessing their practice, seeking out new ideas, and developing personalized action plans, teachers can ensure their classroom management approach remains dynamic, responsive, and effective in meeting the evolving needs of their students.

Through this tireless dedication to honing their craft, teachers create the conditions for transformative learning to occur—where students feel safe, motivated, and equipped to reach their full potential. In classrooms where effective management is the norm, the possibilities for academic achievement, social-emotional development, and overall student thriving are boundless.

ANSWER KEY

CHAPTER 1: INTRODUCTION TO CLASSROOM MANAGEMENT

QUIZ ANSWER 1:

1(D) All of the above

2(C) Reduced teacher stress

3(C) Relationship-based approach

4(C) To meet the diverse needs of all students

5(C) Building upon students' cultural backgrounds and experiences

CHAPTER 2: ESTABLISHING A POSITIVE CLASSROOM

QUIZ ANSWER 2:

1(C) Implementing strict behavior policies

2(B) To promote student ownership and investment

3(B) By modeling acceptance, empathy, and respect

4(D) All of the above

5(D) By treating students with dignity and fairness

CHAPTER 3: DEVELOPING CLASSROOM RULES AND PROCEDURES

QUIZ ANSWER 3:

1(B) To emphasize desired behaviors

2(C) 7

3(A) By displaying the rules and providing regular reminders

4(D) Both a and b

5(C) Understanding the root cause and guiding the student

CHAPTER 4: EFFECTIVE LESSON PLANNING AND INSTRUCTION

QUIZ ANSWER 4:

1(B) To reduce the likelihood of disruptive behaviors

2(D) All of the above

3(C) To meet the diverse needs of all students

4(A) Providing opportunities for "brain breaks"

5(D) Both b and c

CHAPTER 5: MANAGING STUDENT BEHAVIOR

QUIZ ANSWER 5:

1(B) To reduce the likelihood of disruptive behaviors

2(D) All of the above

3(C) To meet the diverse needs of all students

4(A) Providing opportunities for "brain breaks"

5(D) Both b and c

CHAPTER 6: PROMOTING STUDENT ENGAGEMENT AND PARTICIPATION

QUIZ ANSWER 6:

1(A) Creating a stimulating learning environment

2(B) By incorporating natural elements like plants

3(C) Utilizing flexible grouping structures

4(C) Incorporating hands-on experimentation

5(C) It acknowledges and addresses diverse student needs

CHAPTER 7: CLASSROOM ORGANIZATION AND MATERIALS MANAGEMENT

QUIZ ANSWER 7:

1(B) It minimizes distractions and promotes focus

2(C) Whole-group meeting area, individual workspaces, small group collaboration zones, and hands-on exploration stations

3(B) By establishing clear procedures and expectations for material usage

4(B) Prioritizing digital citizenship skills

5(C) Enhancing teaching and learning through strategic technology use

CHAPTER 8: EFFECTIVE COMMUNICATION AND COLLABORATION

QUIZ ANSWER 8:

1(C) It allows for open exchange of information about a child's progress

2(B) By modeling good communication skills

3(C) Involving students in the co-creation of classroom norms

4(B) By facilitating a restorative conversation

5(C) It helps address concerns and disagreements constructively

CHAPTER 9: BUILDING EFFECTIVE CLASSROOM ROUTINES

QUIZ ANSWER 9:

1(C) They provide a sense of structure and stability

2(B) Utilizing countdowns, timers, and nonverbal cues

3(B) They respond quickly and calmly to refocus the class

4(C) To cultivate self-regulation and agency in students

5(C) By incorporating opportunities for student choice and creativity within consistent routines

CHAPTER 10: REFLECTING AND GROWING AS A CLASSROOM MANAGER

QUIZ ANSWER 10:

1(B) It helps teachers identify areas of strength and areas for improvement

2(A) Students, colleagues, and school administrators

3(B) To enhance classroom management skills

4(A) Specific, measurable goals and concrete steps to achieve them

5(B) Because it happens repeatedly over time

www.ingramcontent.com/pod-product-compliance
Lightning Source LLC
LaVergne TN
LVHW070533070526
838199LV00075B/6771